Micro World of
VIRUSES AND
BACTERIA

by Melissa Mayer

CAPSTONE PRESS
a capstone imprint

Published by Capstone Press, an imprint of Capstone
1710 Roe Crest Drive, North Mankato, Minnesota 56003
capstonepub.com

Library of Congress Cataloging-in-Publication Data is available on the Library of Congress
website
ISBN: 9781663976833 (hardcover)
ISBN: 9781666321135 (paperback)
ISBN: 9781666321142 (ebook PDF)

Summary: The world is full of tiny viruses and bacteria that can be seen only through a
microscope. Some bacteria can be helpful, but others make people sick. Viruses can cause
deadly diseases such as COVID-19. Discover all the facts about bacteria and viruses,
including their similarities and differences, how they cause infections, and how people can
keep dangerous germs from spreading.

Editorial Credits
Editor: Arnold Ringstad; Designer: Sarah Taplin; Production Specialists: Joshua Olson and
Laura Manthe

Content Consultant
Tobias Doerr, Assistant Professor, Department of Microbiology, Cornell University

Image Credits
Getty Images: Dr_Microbe, top (spread) 16-17, fpm, Cover; Science Source, 7, 20, TIM
VERNON, 28; Shutterstock: Corona Borealis Studio, 27, Design_Cells, bottom left 19,
Electric Egg, 15, Gorodenkoff, 29, jaddingt, top left 19, Jarun Ontakrai, 10, Kateryna Kon,
top left 9, bottom left 9, 13, Lightspring, middle right 19, nobeastsofierce, 5, peterschreiber.
media, middle right 9, PHOTO JUNCTION, 14, SeventyFour, 23, SweetLeMontea, 25

TABLE OF CONTENTS

Words in **bold** are in the glossary.

MICROSCOPIC BIOLOGY

Some of the smallest things on the planet play huge roles in our lives. These include viruses and bacteria. Some of these tiny things make us sick.

Bacteria and viruses are **microscopic**. Most are way too small to see with the human eye. Scientists measure them in microns. There are 1,000 microns in a millimeter.

Bacteria are usually 0.4 to 10 microns in size. Viruses are usually 0.02 to 0.4 microns across. By comparison, a sheet of aluminum foil is about 18 microns thick. The tip of a sharp pencil is around 500 microns wide.

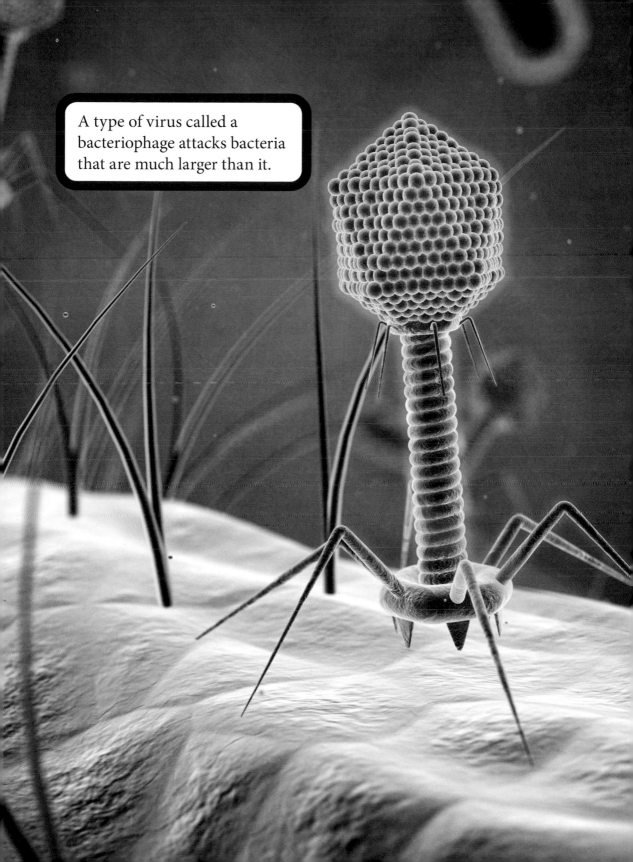

To see bacteria and viruses, scientists use microscopes. A microscope at school might make things look 1,000 times bigger. It's barely possible to see bacteria with these microscopes. But viruses are way too small.

FACT

The very largest bacteria can measure 750 microns across. This is big enough to see with the naked eye.

Antonie van Leeuwenhoek was the first person to see bacteria. He was a scientist in the late 1600s. He invented his own microscopes. In 1683, he scraped white gunk off his teeth and looked at it under the microscope. He saw bacteria zooming around.

Seeing viruses took much longer. Beginning in the late 1800s, a few scientists suspected something smaller than bacteria caused a certain plant disease. The first photos of that virus were finally captured using a high-tech microscope in 1941.

The rod-shaped tobacco mosaic virus was the first virus scientists discovered.

BACTERIA: LIFE AS A SINGLE CELL

Bacteria are about as simple as life gets. They're just one **cell**. In more complicated creatures, each cell has a special compartment that holds **DNA**. But in bacteria, the DNA floats throughout the cell in a clump.

Bacteria come in many shapes. Coccus bacteria are balls. Bacillus bacteria are rods. Some bacteria are shaped like spirals or commas. Others have unusual shapes, like stars. Some even have tails called flagella. The bacteria whip the flagella to move around.

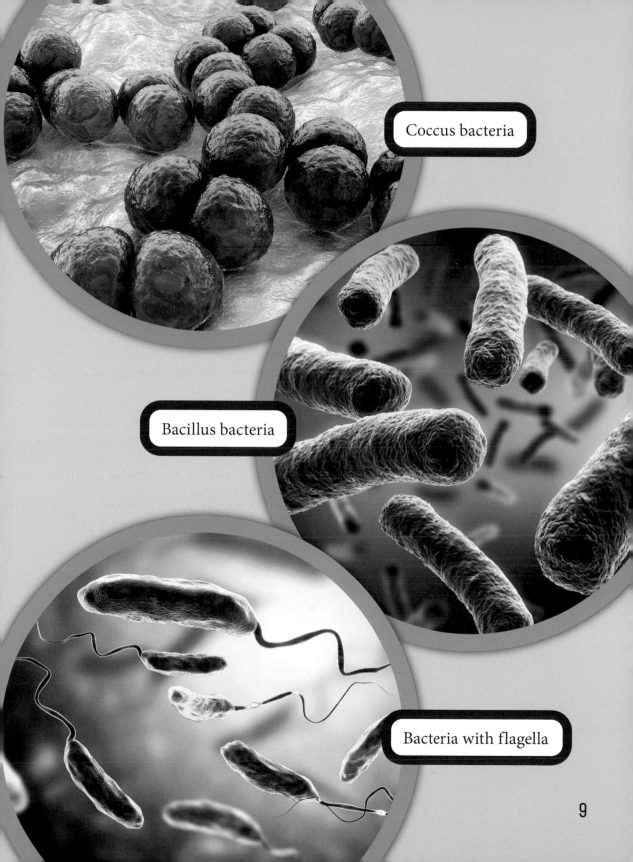

Coccus bacteria

Bacillus bacteria

Bacteria with flagella

In laboratory tests, bacteria colonies can be seen growing in various shapes and patterns.

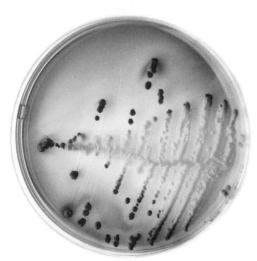
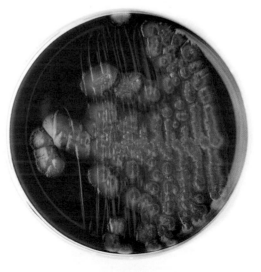

There are about 30,000 known **species** of bacteria. They live practically everywhere. They're in the soil and the oceans. They live high up in the air and deep underground. Some bacteria are **extremophiles**. This means they survive in extreme places. Icy glaciers and underwater volcanoes are no problem for them.

Bacteria reproduce by dividing in half. Each cell can split into two cells. Then those two cells can each split into two more, and so on. All the cells that came from one original cell are known as a colony. Through many rounds of division, the size of a colony can increase quickly.

FACT

Every year the American Society for Microbiology holds an art contest. People grow bacteria in complex designs. They look like paintings!

The human body is home to trillions of bacteria. They live everywhere—on the skin, inside the nose, and in the stomach. There are about 1.5 pounds (0.68 kilograms) of bacteria inside the body of a fourth-grader!

Most bacteria don't bother people. Some are helpful. Bacteria that live in the stomach help break down food. They also make vitamins that help people grow and stay healthy.

Helpful bacteria also boost the immune system. But some medicines kill the body's bacteria. To build them back up, some people take pills filled with bacteria. These are called probiotics.

Useful bacteria live inside the human digestive system.

Bacteria existed before dinosaurs or even plants. Billions of years ago, bacteria in the ocean began turning the sun's energy into nutrients. The bacteria took in a gas called carbon dioxide. They gave off oxygen. That process put vast amounts of oxygen into the air.

Bacteria in the ocean helped make Earth's air breathable for the animals that evolved later.

Bacteria help break down the waste in a compost bin.

Bacteria still have important jobs today. They break down old leaves and dead plants. This releases nutrients that living plants can use. Bacteria also pull a gas called nitrogen from the air. Then they turn it into a form plants can use. Without that nitrogen, many plants couldn't survive.

Some bacteria cause disease. These are known as **pathogens**. Out of millions of species of bacteria, fewer than 1 percent make people sick.

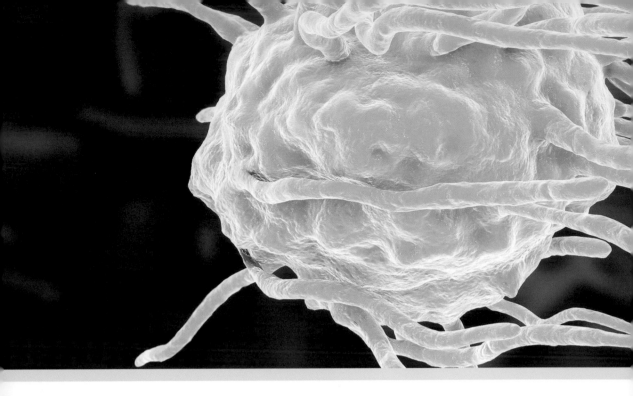

When these bacteria enter the body, they divide quickly. One bacterium can divide into billions in just one day. All those bacteria make it hard for the body's cells to do their jobs. Sometimes the bacteria release **toxins** that harm the body.

The immune system spots harmful bacteria and sends special cells to destroy them. Doctors sometimes prescribe medicines called antibiotics. These kill certain kinds of bacteria.

The white blood cells of the immune system battle against harmful bacteria.

Scientists also make vaccines for diseases caused by bacteria. These shots contain dead or weak bacteria. A vaccine teaches the immune system to recognize the bacteria. That way the immune system can defend against them.

BUBONIC PLAGUE

Bubonic plague is a disease caused by a kind of bacteria carried by rat fleas. In the 1300s, it killed about one-third of all the people in Europe. Today, antibiotics and vaccines keep this disease in check.

VIRUSES: INVADERS OF THE MICRO WORLD

Imagine diving into the ocean and getting a mouthful of seawater. Your mouth would contain water, salt, and around 200 million viruses! Viruses are some of the most common biological objects on the planet.

Scientists do not consider viruses to be living things. They don't eat or make energy. They can't grow or divide on their own. They must invade a living cell to reproduce. Viruses are basically a bundle of DNA or **RNA** inside a protein shell. Some viruses also have an outer coat of fat.

Most viruses are balls or rods. Some have complex shapes. Viruses called phages even look like robot spiders!

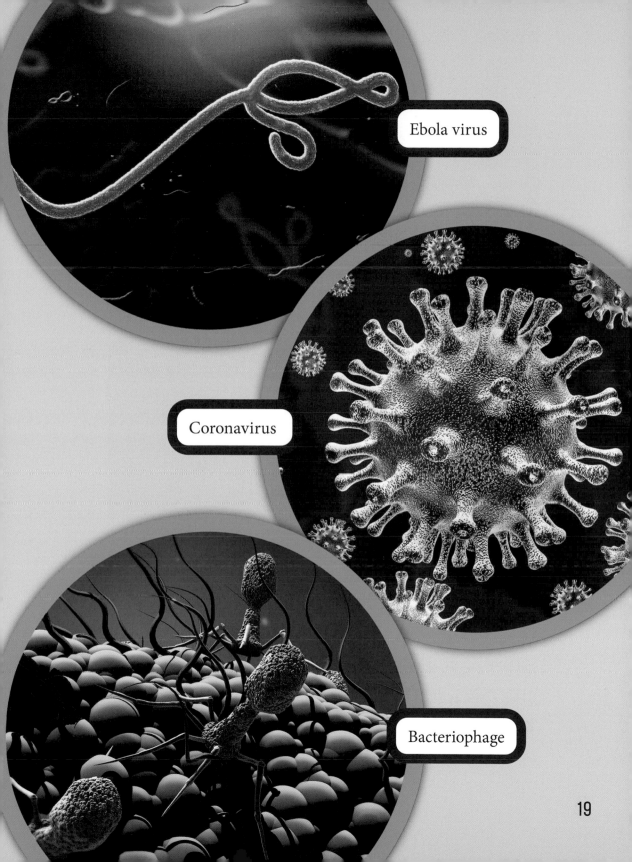

Ebola virus

Coronavirus

Bacteriophage

19

Some viruses can be highly dangerous. Scientists must wear special protective gear to study them.

Viruses are inactive until they bump into the right kind of cell. Then they hook on and break through the cell's outer layer. They inject their **genetic** material into the cell. They use the cell's tools to make copies of themselves. The cell that is invaded is called a host. When the host is full of new viruses, it often bursts open. Each new virus can take over another cell.

Eventually, a virus can make trillions of copies inside a person. They destroy some cells and stop other cells from working properly. This process is what causes an illness. About 200 types of viruses make humans sick.

Many symptoms of sickness are caused by the immune system's reaction to a virus. The immune system raises the body temperature to make it harder for the virus to survive. It sends out chemicals to stop the virus. These reactions can cause symptoms such as fever and body aches.

INSIDE A BIOSAFETY LEVEL 4 LAB

Some scientists study bacteria and viruses that cause deadly diseases. They wear tough plastic suits and masks that provide clean air. They work in labs with special air filtering. The most secure type is a biosafety level 4 lab. Air inside the lab can't escape into the outside world. Scientists must pass through special doors and take showers to leave at the end of the day.

It's tricky to make medicine to kill viruses. All viruses can change over time, and some viruses change very quickly. Every time the virus is copied, there's a chance of a tiny change. Those small changes usually don't matter. But sometimes they make the virus stronger. Some changes even make it harder for the immune system to fight the virus.

ONESIMUS

An enslaved man called Onesimus introduced an early form of vaccination to the United States. Onesimus's real name and earlier life history are unknown. However, around 1716 he told his American enslaver he couldn't get the disease smallpox because he'd had a treatment in West Africa. Some pus from a smallpox sore had been smeared into a cut on his body. This had a similar effect to modern vaccination. The practice saved many lives in Boston after Onesimus explained it to his enslaver.

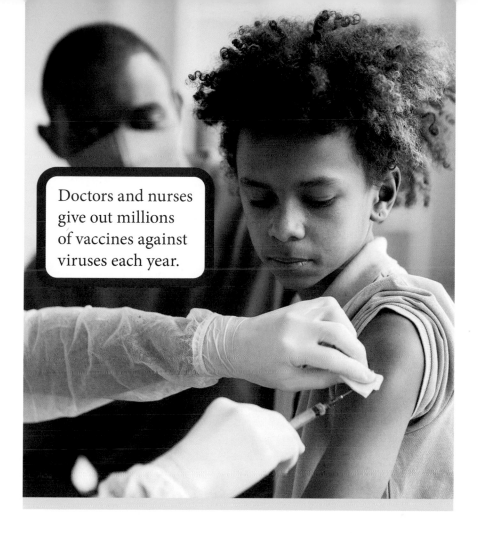

Doctors and nurses give out millions of vaccines against viruses each year.

Just like with bacteria, scientists can make vaccines against viruses. Vaccines teach the immune system how to recognize a virus. Then it can respond if that virus shows up. Some viruses change so fast that scientists make a new vaccine every year. The flu virus is one example.

When people sneeze or cough, tiny droplets fly out. Viruses can spread in these droplets. Other people can breathe in the droplets. Then the virus infects these people. Wearing a face mask can protect against droplets.

Droplets may also land on an object, such as a door handle. They can spread to the next person who touches that object.

Some viruses are spread by animals. For example, insects may carry viruses in their saliva or on their feet. Sometimes people pick up viruses from handling animals, animal poop, or even meat.

FACT

When mosquitoes bite people and suck their blood, these bugs can spread deadly viruses. More than 1 million people die each year from these diseases.

A sneeze can release huge numbers of droplets that contain viruses.

Washing hands helps prevent the spread of viruses and bacteria. That's especially true for viruses with a layer of fat around them. Soap breaks that layer open, destroying the virus.

Some viruses don't burst out of the host cell they invade. Instead, the virus DNA becomes part of the host's DNA.

Scientists think almost one-tenth of human DNA came from viruses. These viruses infected people that lived millions of years ago. Some of that DNA has made humans what we are today.

One example can be seen in the placenta. This organ feeds a developing baby before it's born. The DNA that tells the body to make a placenta came from an ancient virus. Virus DNA may have helped create the complex modern human brain too.

Viruses sometimes change the DNA of the living cells they invade.

Viruses play a role in modern medicine. Scientists have learned how to use viruses like delivery trucks. They can carry pieces of DNA from other viruses into cells. This helps the body learn how to fight off those other viruses. This is how some vaccines work.

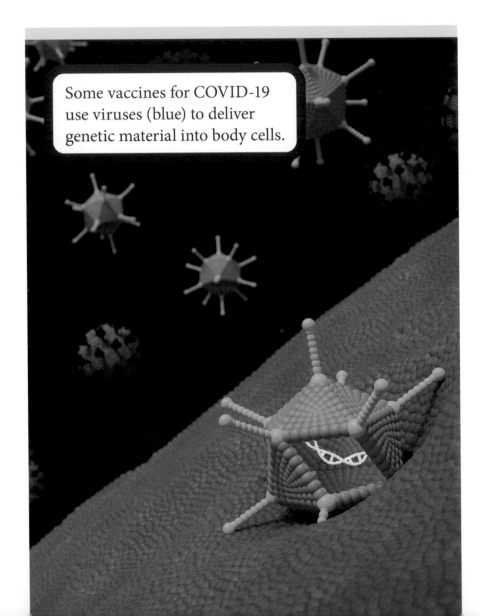

Some vaccines for COVID-19 use viruses (blue) to deliver genetic material into body cells.

Scientists continue to make important new discoveries about viruses and bacteria.

In a similar process, doctors hope to use viruses to fix DNA problems that make people sick. They might even be able to use viruses to attack unhealthy cells, such as cancer cells.

The micro world of viruses and bacteria can be hard to imagine. These things are amazingly small. We need special equipment to see them. Still, they have been crucial in shaping the world we know today.

GLOSSARY

cell (SELL)—a basic building block that makes up a living thing

DNA (dee-en-A)—short for deoxyribonucleic acid, a double-stranded molecule inside a living thing that includes instructions for that living thing's traits

extremophile (ex-TREE-muh-file)—a creature that thrives in very harsh conditions

genetic (juh-NEH-tik)—related to the instructions found in an organism's DNA or RNA

microscopic (my-kruh-SKAH-pik)—too small to see with the unaided human eye

pathogen (PA-thuh-juhn)—a bacterium or other tiny organism that causes disease

RNA (arr-en-A)—short for ribonucleic acid, a single-stranded molecule inside a living thing that includes instructions for that living thing's traits

species (SPEE-sheez)—a group of similar creatures that can reproduce together

toxin (TOCK-sin)—a poison

READ MORE

Biskup, Agnieszka. *Understanding Viruses with Max Axiom, Super Scientist*. North Mankato, MN: Capstone, 2019.

Moon, Walt K. *The COVID-19 Virus*. San Diego, CA: BrightPoint Press, 2021.

Mould, Steve. *The Bacteria Book*. New York: DK, 2018.

INTERNET SITES

Britannica Kids: Virus
kids.britannica.com/kids/article/virus/390098

DK Find Out!: Germs and Disease
dkfindout.com/us/human-body/body-defenses/germs-and-disease/

KidsHealth: What Are Germs?
kidshealth.org/en/kids/germs.html

INDEX

ABOUT THE AUTHOR

Melissa Mayer is a science writer and former science teacher who's currently working on an M.S. in Entomology. She lives on a tiny urban homestead in Portland, Oregon, with her wife, kids, and way too many animals—dogs, cats, rabbits, chickens, and an ever-growing collection of insects. She's the author of five nonfiction books for children and young adults.